THE
NEW YORKER

CARTOON
ALBUM

1975—1985

THE
NEW YORKER

CARTOON
ALBUM

1975—1985

PENGUIN BOOKS

PENGUIN BOOKS
Viking Penguin Inc., 40 West 23rd Street,
New York, New York 10010, U.S.A.
Penguin Books Ltd, 27 Wrights Lane, London W8 5TZ
(Publishing & Editorial) and Harmondsworth,
Middlesex, England (Distribution & Warehouse)
Penguin Books Australia Ltd, Ringwood,
Victoria, Australia
Penguin Books Canada Limited, 2801 John Street,
Markham, Ontario, Canada L3R 1B4
Penguin Books (N.Z.) Ltd, 182–190 Wairau Road,
Auckland 10, New Zealand

First published in the United States of America by
Viking Penguin Inc. 1985
Published in Penguin Books 1987

Design and layout by Joseph Carroll, John Murphy, and Bernard
McAteer of *The New Yorker* staff

LIBRARY OF CONGRESS CATALOGING IN PUBLICATION DATA
The New Yorker cartoon album, 1975–1985.
Cartoons originally published in the New Yorker.
1. American wit and humor, Pictorial.   I. New
Yorker (New York, N.Y.: 1925)
NC1428.N454   1987   741.5'973   87-10583
ISBN 0 14 00.8111 9

Printed in the United States of America by
Murray Printing Company, Westford, Massachusetts
Set in Caslon Old Face No. 2

THE
NEW YORKER

CARTOON
ALBUM

1975—1985

"The thing I like about New York, Claudia, is you."

"*Good night, and thanks for allowing us into your living room.*"

*"Maynard, I do think that just this once you should
come out and see the moon!"*

"Ezra, I'm not inviting you to my birthday party, because our relationship
is no longer satisfying to my needs."

*"There are few moments in music so thrilling as when Brucie
and Mrs. Ritterhouse start riffing in tandem."*

"Did you hear what happened to King Kong?"

"Please, sir, I want some more."

"It's agreed, then, that we dispense with the reading of the minutes and proceed directly to new business."

"But can they save themselves?"

"For God's sake, stop picking at it!"

"She's all work and no play."

"You've been selected to appear in the forthcoming edition of 'Who's Who on the Lone Prairie.'"

"Why, it isn't gingerbread at all! It's just plain old pumpernickel."

"Gee!"

"Hey! 'Made in U.S.A.'!"

"Don't panic. I'm just a sore throat."

"*Please, Mrs. Enright, if I let you pinch-hit for Tommy, all the mothers will want to pinch-hit.*"

"*I see by the current issue of 'Lab News,' Ridgeway, that you've been working for the last twenty years on the same problem I've been working on for the last twenty years.*"

"We were here ten years ago. That was the time we went to Harry's Bar
and Roger fell in the Grand Canal."

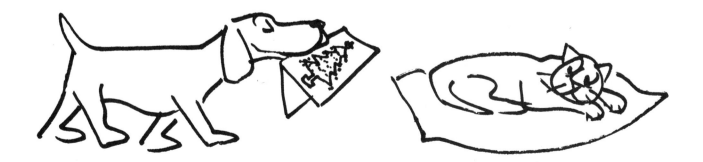

"Alden, which of the five senses do you value most?"

"On the other hand, we've had a lot of wonderful years in the tourist business."

OLD COUPLES

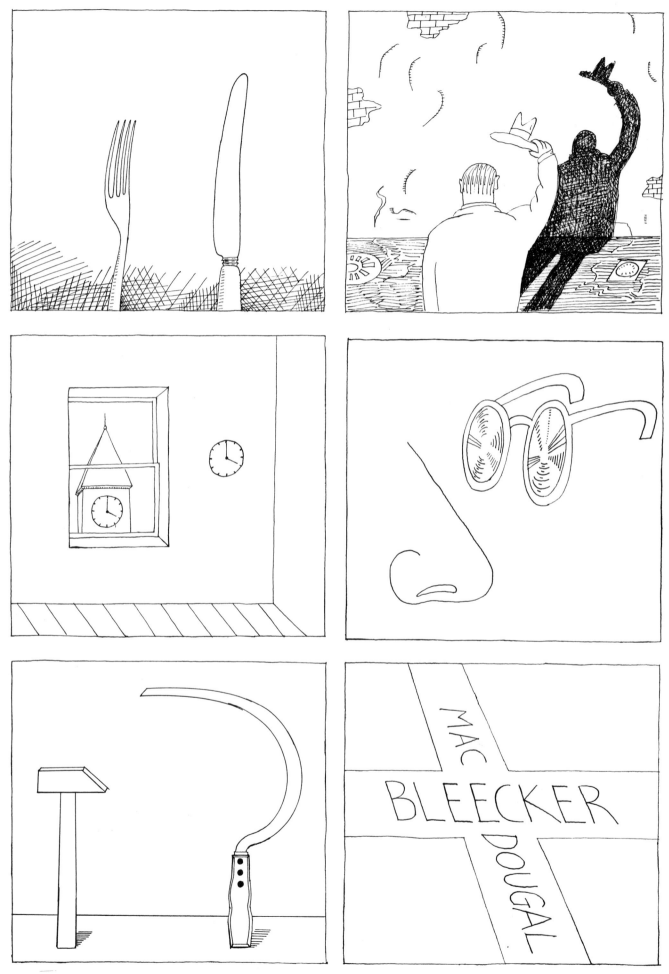

BEES

WORKER QUEEN

DRONE CONSULTANT

"Stop me if you've heard this one."

"I read 'Art News.'"

O'BRIAN

"In Larchmont! Well, really!"

FOUR HUNDRED SELECTIONS OF THE WORLD'S FINEST ORCHESTRAL MUSIC, OVER ONE THOUSAND FULL-COLOR REPRODUCTIONS OF MANKIND'S GREATEST PAINTINGS AND SCULPTURE, AND TWO HUNDRED AND THIRTY-ONE TIMELESS CLASSICS OF WESTERN LITERATURE COMPACTED INTO A TWO-BY-THREE-BY-SIX-INCH BRICK.

"Have a pious, thrifty, hardworking day."

"May I interject a note of caution?"

"It's only the wind."

"It's hard to believe that everything _doesn't_ have a military solution."

HAUTE CUISINE

NOUVELLE CUISINE

CUISINE VÉRITÉ

Stuart Leeds

"What about that day in 1922 when you said 'Shut up' to your mother?"

KEEPING WARM

Heated
BB boots.
← CORK
Sew canvas boots. Slip on over shoes.

Fill with hot BBs.
BBs heat fast in an iron skillet.

On sunny cold days, carry clothes in suitcase and quickly pinch on Kitchen-foil suit.

Turkey pan (foil $1.29) will work best for quick Pinch-on cap.

Heated tire irons wrapped in towels can be carried under one's topcoat.

Hot-water tie.
Warm all day at the office.

Face catnip comforter.

"Does it strike anyone else as weird that none of the great painters have ever been men?"

"We might make unwise international loans, Mr. Simpson,
but we don't make unwise loans to individuals."

LITE® BOOKS

Madame Bovary LITE®

Madame B., dissatisfied with her lot in life, goes on a shopping spree. Later, she returns everything but a hat.

Anna Karenina LITE®

Anna K., a married woman, has a date with a Count Vronsky. He moves away, and they never see each other again.

Crime and Punishment LITE®

Raskolnikov writes a nasty letter to a pawnbroker, but later feels guilty and apologizes.

R. Chast

"Is it too cutesy?"

"Look, will you forget about them? They're in the past. The important thing is what I feel now—about you!"

"Have you got something a little more . . . hard-nosed?"

"Anything wrong?"

"Captain, this Brie is totally out of control!"

"This is Ronnie Lawson, Dad. Ronnie has a .310 lifetime batting average."

"Come on. It's late."

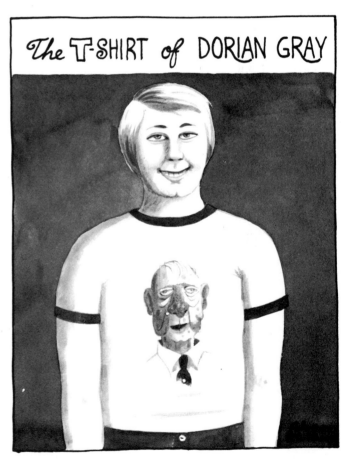

The T-SHIRT of DORIAN GRAY

"We were very unhappy in England."

"*You may switch to the less expensive wine now.*"

"Et cetera, et cetera, et cetera."

ALTERNATIVE SPACES

Pothole Estates

Junior Studio

Two-Bedroom Kayak

Basement Single

Eight-Bedroom Walkthrough

Packing-Crate Loft

Dumpster Duplex

"I'm sorry to interrupt the più mosso, but Mrs. Patterson
informs me the cat has passed away."

"Inevitably, I find, I fall in love with guys named Thor, and then, just as inevitably, I dump them."

"And what do you do to maintain your cardiovascular fitness, Miss Holt?"

"Son, you're all grown up now. You owe me two hundred and fourteen thousand dollars."

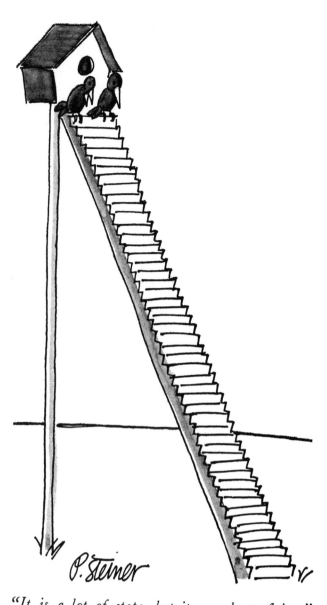

"It _is_ a lot of steps, but it sure beats flying."

"Ed used to be an incurable optimist, but now he's cured."

"I dreamed Malcolm Forbes took me up in his balloon."

LITTLE HOUSE ON THE PRAIRIE

"Save some for me, Fatso."

"Gentlemen, being a superpower is no longer enough. We must become a super-duper power."

"When I was a kid, I had a box of wooden soldiers, and I thought the world of those soldiers. Somehow I lost them, and it nearly broke my little heart. Well, my old mother says to me, 'Never mind, lad. You'll find your wooden soldiers again someday.'"

"B. K. Howley here—cordless."

"Well. That's more like it!"

"Your car will be right down, Mr. Lundquist."

"I know it doesn't look that great now, but once you accessorize it with the right jewelry, I guarantee you the whole 'Mr. T' look will fall into place."

"He'll be a year old at Easter."

"*Before proceeding, Gertrude will read the minutes of the last Thanksgiving.*"

"You're a good man, Washbourne. I like the way you use nouns as verbs."

"The jury will disregard the witness's last remarks."

"I'm sorry, Travers, but I'm going to have to let you go."

THE RACHMANINOFF FILE

First the strange mixup with the baggage and the prattle of the boorish Count Deschamps. Now customs was impounding his Beretta. Still, Holcomb Travis was determined to let nothing spoil his holiday.

The urgent summons to the cabaret proved to be a false alarm. But there was Gillian Lathrop. A delightful coincidence—or was it?

When the body of Sir Alistair Royce was discovered sprawled between the neat rows of Chassagne-Montrachet, Herman Laubrich had already disappeared, to no one's surprise.

They were all there in the dining salon: Baron Rosenwasser, Herr Klimt, Mrs. Parsegian, and the Marburgs. As he studied the wine list, all the pieces seemed to fit into place.

Serge Katzourakis was followed every-where by the obsequious Mr. Waxman. Were they actually father and son?

The usually taciturn Frau Berthe had been oddly insistent about changing his towels at precisely 11:25. Normally, she changed the Hochfelds' towels at 11:25.

If Prager had not bent forward at that moment to retrieve Professor Hensle's lighter, the runaway ski would have brought the pursuit to a grisly conclusion.

Inspector Forsythe observed that Dr. Kesselman had been asleep in the lounge when Mme. Fleischer was attacked, and also when the mail arrived. He was there still.

Just as the warning whistle blew, he became aware of two figures racing through the steam toward the Trans-Europe Express. Suddenly he knew the answer. But was it too late?

"I *love* the Caribbean in February!"

"If it's not the goddam summer people, it's the goddam winter people!"

"Yes, sir, it's made right here in this country with Japanese know-how."

"Miss Slinsky, I smell money. Check it out, will you?"

"That's the trouble with pets. They're so destructive."

"I *beg* your pardon."

"Have you said goodbye to the children?"

"*What have you done to yourself, Hank? You somehow look forty years younger.*"

"*What it boils down to, Sire, is that they seek a life style more similar to your own.*"

*"It *is* a superb vision of America, all right, but I can't remember which candidate projected it."*

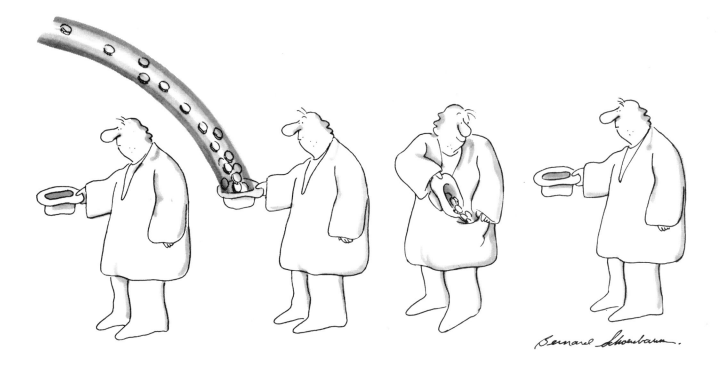

"*And the winner is Anton Schmegler, Sourball of the Year.*"

Anthony

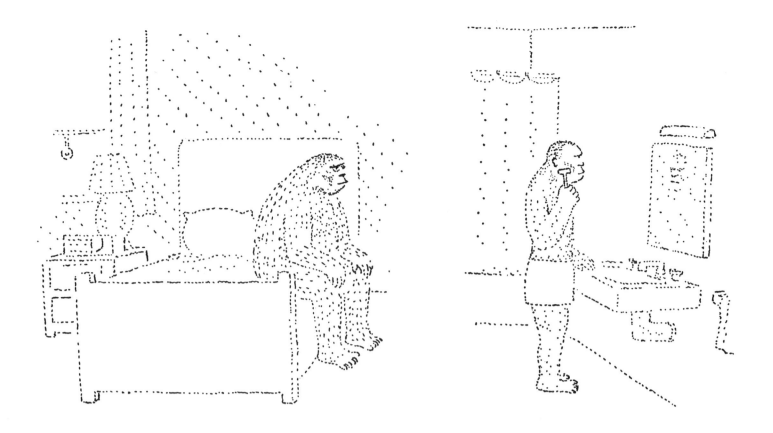

*"Too bad about old Ainsworth. Published and published,
but perished all the same."*

Last Row: Scott, Jennifer, Jennifer, Scott, Jennifer, Jennifer, Scott, Scott
Middle Row: Jennifer, Jennifer, Scott, Scott, Jennifer, Jennifer, Scott, Jennifer, Scott *Front Row:* Jennifer, Scott, Scott, Jennifer, Mrs. Wanda Projhieki, Scott, Scott, Scott, Scott

"This song describes the events of a lovely spring day. The sky is a cloudless blue, birds are singing, and out at the ballpark the grass is an emerald green. It's the top of the fourth, there are two out and runners on first and second. The batter hits a slow roller down the third-base line. The third baseman scoops up the ball barehanded and tries for a force play at second . . ."

"*Mr. Edwards, this is your secretary, Melissa. When you have a moment, would you run down and get me a regular coffee and a pineapple Danish?*"

The Frog Prince calls on the Princess.

The Beast proposes to Beauty.

The Witch greets Hansel and Gretel.

The Queen "guesses" Rumpelstiltskin's name.

"O.K., now Reed, Bruno, Parker & Van Patten, Inc., followed by Hanover, Norris, Upham, Wallace & Peck."

"People who can laugh at themselves, Marguerite, do so and fall by the wayside."

"Damn! I suppose this means another malpractice suit!"

"Miss Jenkins, would you please bring a round object into my office?"

"Thank God! A panel of experts!"

"Sorry, sir."

"First I was a 'non-candidate,' then I was a 'potential candidate,' and now I'm an 'ex-candidate.' Didn't we miss a step somewhere?"

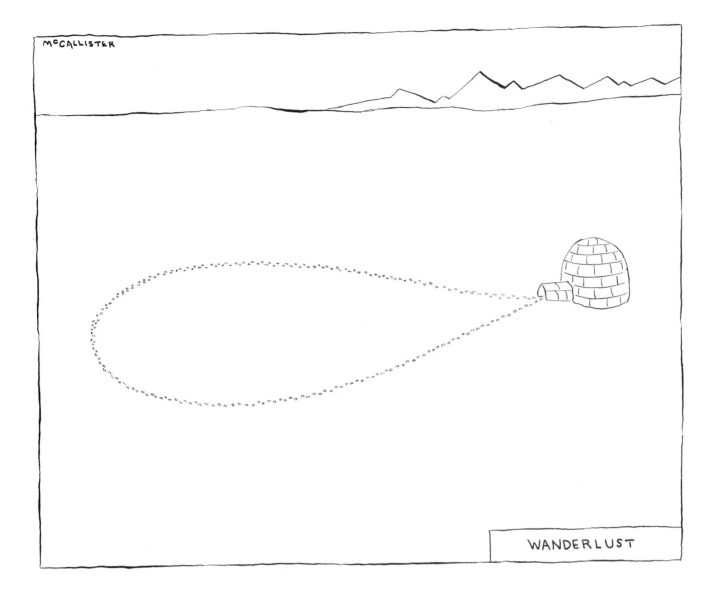

McCALLISTER

WANDERLUST

"It's been up two days. If there are no damn birds
by tomorrow, down it comes!"

"I don't see _my_ picture around here anywhere."

STAR

RATS

STEINBERG

KOREN

"*Here to share their thoughts and feelings with us this evening are Jackie Parsons-Wilder, Eugenia Robbins-Randolph, Sarah Brundelmeyer-Hurd, Rachel Rice-Grant, and Jane Thomaston-Whitehouse-Morgenthaller.*"

"Bob up and down."

"I agree he's a homicidal maniac, but I'm saluting the office, not the man."

"Why, no, Ken—I don't want to talk about it."

"Honey, I'm home!"   *"Honey, I'm home!"*

"Look who's up for the weekend again."

"The zucchini's in!"

"For heaven's sake! When did you have your ear pierced?"

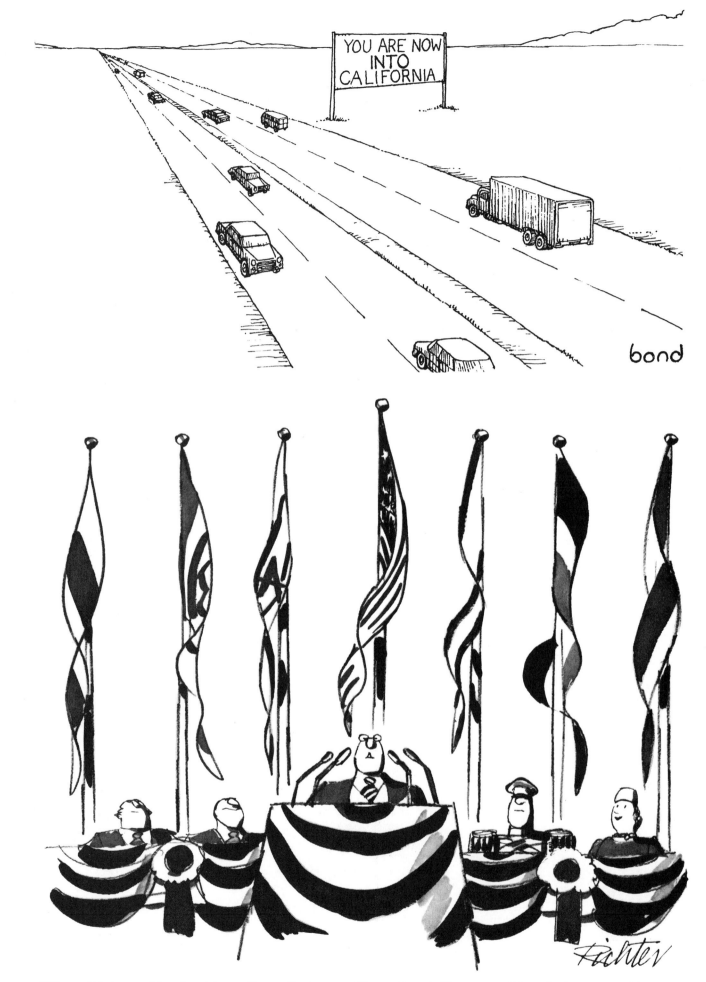

"*Your Majesty, Mr. President, Your Eminence, Your Royal Highness, Mr. Ambassador, Madam Chairperson, Your Excellency, distinguished clergy, most gracious host, fellow-delegates, loyal supporters, comrades-in-arms, honorable fellows, most generous sponsors, honored patrons, distinguished guests, kind friends, fellow-countrymen, ladies and gentlemen— And now I see my time is up.*"

"Thomas Cole!"　　　　"Here!"
"Asher Durand!"　　　"Yo!"
"Frederick Church!"　"Present!"
"John Kensett!"　　　"Here!"

"'Stocks drifted gently to a lower plateau.' Why, that's very poetic, isn't it?"

"And now, for all of you out there who are in love, or if you've ever been in love, or if you think you'll be in love someday, or even if you only think you might like to be in love someday, this song is for you."

"There it is again, Louie. Didn't you hear a car honk?"

More Hamptons

Tubhampton

Fanhampton

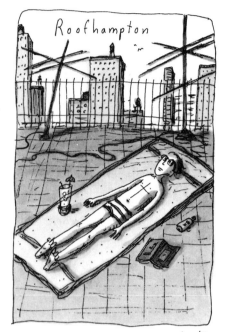

Roofhampton

R. Chast

"Look, lady, if it's trendy you want, Bloomie's is at Fifty-ninth and Lex."

FORBIDDEN APPETITES

wMiller

"Write about dogs!"

"What do you mean 'Your guess is as good as mine'? My guess is a hell of a lot _better_ than your guess!"

PLUMBING TROUBLE OF THE GODS

"Stop bouncing bits of trivia off people."

"Well, gentlemen, Christmas is over."

"Hey, look! A congressman!"

Bernard Schoenbaum.

"I knew about the wings, but the webbed feet are a surprise."

*"General Hoskins, I don't care if you <u>are</u> in charge of our
star-wars defense. You must wear a regulation uniform."*

UNPROVOKED ASSAULTS

The Dust Ball

The Casually Tossed
Piece of Popcorn

The Surprising Jalapeño
Pepper Hors d'Oeuvre

Noon

The New Hairdo Grazing the Wind Chimes

The Inexplicable Henny Youngman
Monologue Over Muzak

"I love you, and I want you to be my bird."

"Well, Koch is at least right about the middle class. I think we're a pretty terrific bunch."

"Gentlemen, let us pool our expertise."

LEXINGTON AVENUE

GRAMERCY PARK

AT 28TH STREET (APPROX.)

CHRYSLER BUILDING AT 42ND STREET

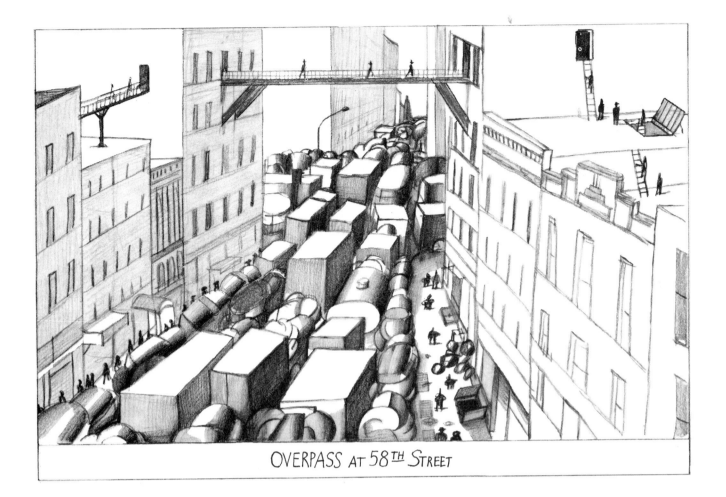

OVERPASS AT 58TH STREET

67TH STREET

LENOX HILL at 73RD STREET

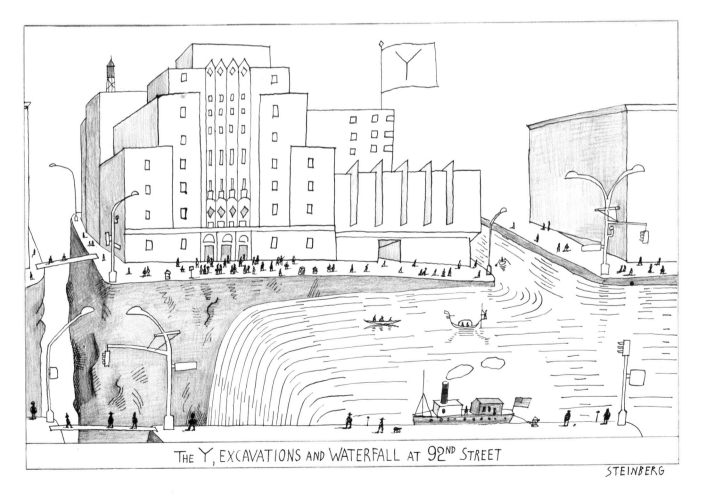

THE Y, EXCAVATIONS AND WATERFALL AT 92ND STREET

STEINBERG

"*I don't know whether mortgage rates had gone up. Now may I continue?*"

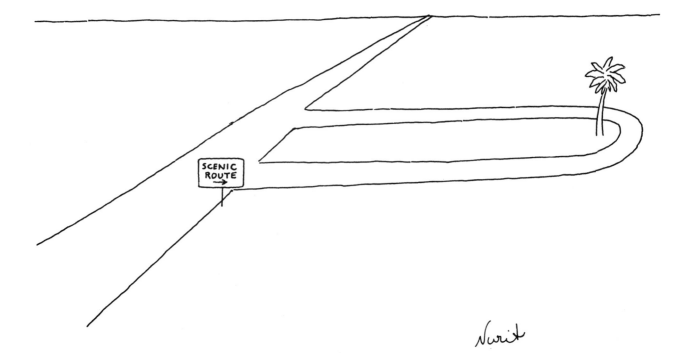

"Hey, a *whale*! I mean thar she blows!"

"Ground floor, gentlemen. Happy trails."

"*Dear Diary:*
Parades, concerts, dancing, banquets, gala balls, fireworks. Today is my birthday, and the whole kingdom is making quite a fuss over it."

"My net worth happens to be none of your business!"

"I was at my sister's today. They have two pots."

"You were sensational."

ROGET'S BRONTOSAURUS

"Scarsdale. It's Scarsdale again."

"Beethoven is working on his Eight-Hundred-and-Forty-seventh Symphony, but I still prefer the Ninth."

"It's the multitude, and they're _not_ singing
'For He's a Jolly Good Fellow.'"

"Push the Scotch salmon with dill sauce."

"Evolution's been good to you, Sid."

"David never gives up. I used to think that was a virtue."

"Good news. The 'Times' has upgraded us from a 'junta' to a 'military government.'"

"I suppose you know you're spoiling that dog."

"Admiral Terence Northrup and his wife, the Mary-Esther."

"Are you from the neighborhood, sir?
We're a neighborhood bank."

"Sorry, sir, but there's a party
of four ahead of you."

"I would have recognized you anywhere, Mr. Davis.
You look exactly like your corporation."

"Sure you were my sunshine, but you weren't my _only_ sunshine!"

"Hi, kids! Want a lift?"

"Ah! The people versus Herman Pretzfelder."

WHY THEY HAVE SPRING TRAINING

OH, HELL.

"I find there's a lot of pressure to be good."

"Nothing serious. I just couldn't bring myself to give thanks for the corn pudding."

"Touché, Hadley. You're fired."

"Do you know what would be nice, Matthew? It would be nice if we had a few firecrackers."

"Tom, young Mr. Moncure here is that Harvard M.B.A. I was telling you about who has the keen sense of depreciation."

"How would you guys feel if I gave all this
up and went on Social Security?"

"Would you please have the orchestra play
'Tea for Two,' and I'll just have tea for
one, thank you."

"I'm the Raider Fedora on the extreme left."

NED'S CONSUMER HOT LINE

Dear Ned,
   Boy, am I steamed! About 3 days ago, I sent Acme Pencils 11¢, and I _never_ got my pencil. What should I do?

   Steamed-up Guy

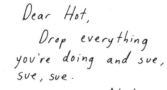

Dear Ned,
   Recently, while I was sharpening an Acme pencil, the point simply fell out. Any advice?

   Hot Under the Collar

Dear Ned,
   Soon after I received my Acme pencil (11¢), it rolled off the desk and onto the floor. Upon retrieving it, I hit my head on the desk. Can I hold Acme responsible?

   Boiling Mad

Dear Steamed,
   Sue them for everything they've got.
   Ned

Dear Hot,
   Drop everything you're doing and sue, sue, sue.
   Ned

Dear Boiling,
   This is what's known as an open-and-shut case. If you don't sue them, I will.
   Ned

"Just what exactly is the difference between a goblin and a hobgoblin?"

"To be perfectly frank, I'm not nearly as smart as you seem to think I am."

CHRISTIANSON

"So, Benson—this is how you spend your lunch hour!"

"There are five elements, son—earth, air, fire, water, and women."

"When Alexander the Great stopped here, we thought the town would take off. But it didn't."

TO FEED MY BROTHER:
FOUR NAVAJO CORN ORIGIN MYTHS

Chief Andrew Real Bird discovers corn at the Grand Union.

A Navajo gets some corn from a guy.

John He Throws Them in the Water receives a free sample of corn in the mail.

Isaac Six Ponies meets corn at a mixer.

DISCOVERING THAT THE LIGHT AT THE
END OF THE TUNNEL IS NEW JERSEY

"*I have distressing news, ladies and gentlemen. It seems
<u>we</u> have been penetrated by the Mob.*"

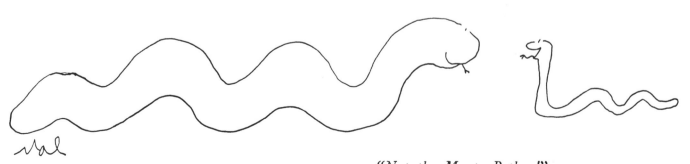

"*Not <u>the</u> Monty Python!*"

"Don't you think we've already been to one crafts fair too many?"

JOSEPH FARRIS

"*I'm sorry, Mel, but we're letting all our anchormen go.
Our viewers don't want any more news.*"

"Check your wheel, sir?"

"Your Majesty, according to our study the shoe was lost for want of a nail,
the horse was lost for want of a shoe, and the rider was lost for want of a horse,
but the _kingdom_ was lost because of overregulation."

"We located the hissing noise, Mr. Watkins. Your wife's mother is in the back seat."

A Dream of Chicken Soup

"Damn it, I love you, don't you understand? How can you just sit there and read when you know how much I love you and want to go for a walk?"

"Is there anyone in the house who can sing Siegfried?"

"What do you consider your biggest fault, and what are you going to do about it?"

TWO ROADS DIVERGED IN A WOOD AND I... I... I... SOB...

"Why can't you get one of those stationary bicycles, like everyone else?"

"We regret the inconvenience, sir. We are experiencing technical difficulties. Please stand by."

"How about one of those sunny old grandpas who make things look honest?"

"Oh, my God! We forgot Tobago!"

"Would you excuse me, Miss Arkwright? I just remembered that I promised to forsake all others."

"Here you go, boys. Two Perrier-and-lime, one
chilled white wine, and a Tab."

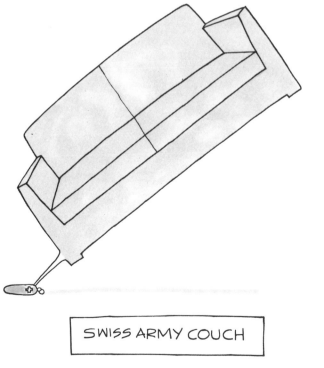

SWISS ARMY COUCH

"Wornal, take this plant out and kill it."

"I wish someone would take
him out to the ballgame and leave him there."

"*Attention, please. At 8:45 A.M. on Tuesday, July 29, 2008, you are all scheduled to take the New York State bar exam.*"

"Here's the story, gentlemen. Sometime last night, an eleven-year-old kid in Akron, Ohio, got into our computer and transferred all our assets to a bank in Zurich."

Folklorist

"Would you have a moment, dear, to share
Ivy's dissatisfaction?"

"*Arthur, I think I liked our little nest better before we put in track lighting.*"

"You majored in English, Brinwell. Write us up a nice
little request for higher appropriations."

"Nothing happens next. This is it."

"*I hate to admit it, but I got that information from Phil Donahue's show.*"

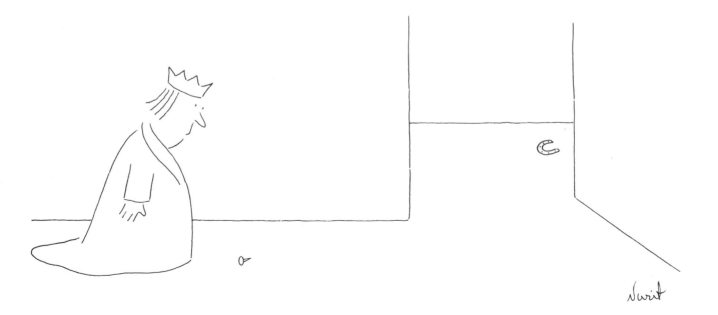

"*In a moment we'll have a few words by the chairman of the board. But, first, Mahler's Eighth Symphony.*"

"Oh, Kate, Kate, Kate. I don't like the name Kate."

"Well, I like it five to one!"

"All right, Wilhelm, we have the child walking through the woods."

"Woods are always good, Wilhelm. Now, who does the child meet?"

"We *did* that, Wilhelm."

"Please, Jacob, don't you think we've been using the woods too much?"

"Perhaps a dwarf or two?"

"How about a wolf, Jacob?"

"Sorry about this, but I just ran out of sand."

"Call me a sentimental fool, but I <u>still</u> worship the almighty dollar."

"That's a cloud, too. They're all clouds."

"That's Mr. Brock. He didn't have a happy New Year, a happy Valentine's Day, a happy St. Patrick's Day, a happy Easter, a happy Father's Day, a happy Halloween, a happy Thanksgiving, or a merry Christmas. He <u>did</u> have, however, a safe and sane Fourth of July."

" '_No!_' shouted Mr. Bixbey, slamming his fist down on the table. The floor shook, the walls trembled. Mr. Watson turned ashen. 'Y-y-you m-m-mean w-w-we . . .' The words wouldn't come out. He seemed to choke on each syllable."

"Go to bed, Osgood! You've had enough!"

"I love the texture of life aboard ship."

CORPORATE-SPONSORED BIOGRAPHIES OF THE GREAT

When young Pablo arrived in Paris, he was amazed at the variety of wallpapers he had to choose from.
—"The Youth of Pablo Picasso"
©1975, International Wallpaper Institute

Fëdor smiled grimly, knowing that the future of his hard-earned dacha, troika, and samovar depended on this next roll. He stepped forward and sent the ball on its way home.
—"Dostoevski's Luck"
©1969, United States of America Bowling Association

Karl glanced at the last stick of beef jerky on his plate. He longed to savor it through these final difficult paragraphs of the book that would bring him both fame and obloquy.
—"Capitalism and Lunch: The Secret Life of Karl Marx"
©1973, Beefy Snax Corporation

Freud lay down on the lounge chair. The gentle buzzing of the mosquitoes soon lulled him to sleep, and he dreamed a dream that would change the face of psychology forever.
—"Interpretation of Freud"
©1958, Lawn Chairs Unlimited of Pasadena

Although Fiorello LaGuardia and Albert Einstein laughed and laughed and laughed at the joke, their socks did not fall down.
—"A Remarkable Friendship"
©1971, He-Man Hose Manufacturing Company

Villa readjusted his sunglasses against the blazing Mexican noon and stared out across the vast expanse. "So this is it," he murmured. "The whole enchilada."
—"Pancho Villa: The Action Years"
©1963, Sun-Ban Company

"I'm an old-fashioned private eye, Miss Jones. If this little mystery of yours has anything to do with computers, forget it."

"Before we get under way, just who is this Michael Jackson?"

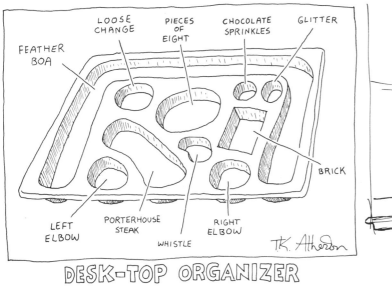

FEATHER
BOA

LOOSE
CHANGE

PIECES
OF
EIGHT

CHOCOLATE
SPRINKLES

GLITTER

BRICK

LEFT
ELBOW

PORTERHOUSE
STEAK

WHISTLE

RIGHT
ELBOW

DESK-TOP ORGANIZER

"*This is only a test.*"

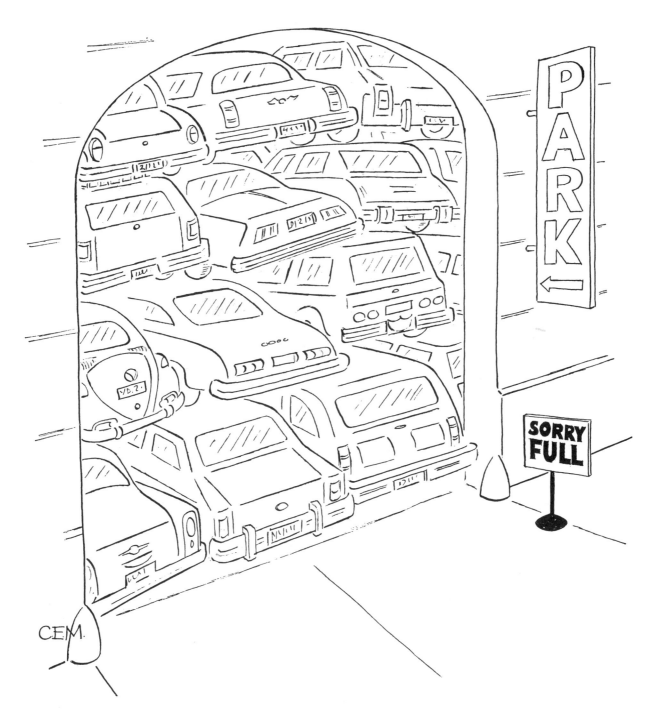

"It's the 'Love Boat,' sir. Shall we let her have it?"

"Some women to see you, Anne."

"*What a delightful surprise. I always thought it just trickled down to the poor.*"

"*It was right where you left it—under the table.*"

"Please, Doris, let's talk!"

ITINERARY			
	DRINKS	EATS	
N.Y.	🍷 🍷	🥧	LOOK AROUND
	DRINKS	EATS	
N.J.	🍷 🍷	🥧	LOOK AROUND
	DRINKS	EATS	
MARS	🍷 🍷	🥧	LOOK AROUND

"I don't know why everybody complains about how the Pentagon spends its money. If they had any idea how hard Keatley works to save money for everyone concerned, they would thank their lucky stars to have a man like him doing what he does in the Pentagon. Lucille, he takes those fourteen- and fifteen-year-old Vietnam airplanes, assigns them to our Air National Guard units for a while, and then eventually sells them to a little-bitty Central American ally for eight hundred thousand dollars each. That's the kind of money Keatley is saving every day. Every day, Lucille! And, of course, the little-bitty ally doesn't pay a dime of that, either, because Keatley and the Pentagon have all those details worked out in advance with the Congress."

"All right, food people—are you ready?"

"Surprise!"

"Superb Martinis!"

"By the way, Harrison—you, too."

"Gutsy lady, meet another gutsy lady!"

ENTERING
GRANOLA
—
THE HEALTH CITY

"Son, your mother is a remarkable woman."

"We are gathered here today to honor all major credit cards."

BACK HOME AGAIN
IN INDIANA

"Don't tell me. You've left Roy. Your brother arrived this morning. He's left Joyce. It's going to be an old-fashioned Christmas after all."

"Even a small kingdom, Your Highness, can make effective use of modern management techniques."

HEY! THANKS!

OUT OF TOWNER

THE DARK SIDE OF THE LONE RANGER

WHAT AM I TALKING, TONTO? CHOPPED LIVER? **NO!** I'M TALKING SILVER BULLETS!

I DON'T CARE **HOW** YOU GET THEM, DAMMIT — JUST **GET** THEM!

"Do you know everybody? Actor-director Russell Bain, songwriter-producer Sandy Whitley, actress-model Monique D'Amie, dancer-singer Alicia Kelly, writer-producer Bartley Smail . . ."

"To living very New York but feeling very California!"

*"Nobody came to work today, Mr. Farvis, because today
is a national holiday. Today is Christmas."*

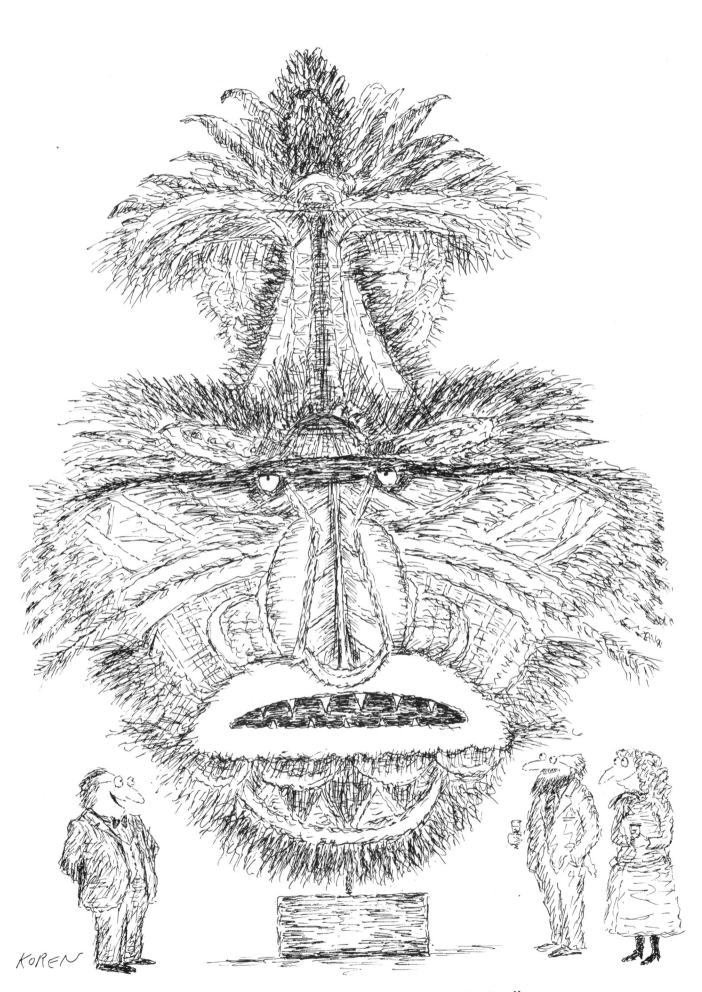

"Its mere possession is immensely satisfying."

"This is Chuck Whartley and the TBC News team signing off."

"Oh, Lord! Not _another_ wine-and-cheese party."

"There. I've written all the checks for the month. I feel cleansed."

"Little Susie Miller all grown up."

"Everything that was bad for you is now good for you."

"Did Yogi Berra ever say anything besides 'It ain't over till it's over'?"

"Turgid. I love it."

"It's all right, dear. Kidder, Peabody. For me."

"Teacher burnout."

sempé.

"911! 911!"

FELLOW MEN

Woman Reading Love Letter

*Pedestrian Catching Reflection
in Store Window*

*Freighter Headed for
Nearest Port*

*Subway Rider in a
Staring Duel*

The Elderly Suitor

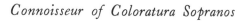

Connoisseur of Coloratura Sopranos

"*You know, I find it increasingly difficult to believe that you were born in Dallas.*"

"Sure I'm depressed. I haven't hit a grand-slam home run in twenty-seven years."

"I'm sorry, dear, but you knew I was a bureaucrat when you married me."

"I understand you perfectly, Harold. When you say you want to extend your parameters, it means you want floozies."

"Quick! Your gut reaction."

"I'm absolutely against total war, but then
I'm not for total peace, either."

"He-e-e-e-e-e-e-e-e-e-ere's Johnny!
He-e-e-e-e-e-e-e-e-e-ere's Johnny!
He-e-e-e-e-e-e-e-e-e-ere's Johnny!
He-e-e-e-e-e-e-e-e-e-ere's Johnny!"

"Do you realize we are living through the second time
people got tired of Art Deco?"

RECIPES
from the
AMERICAN CHEESE COUNCIL

Cheese Omelette

2 eggs
5 lb. Swiss cheese
1 tbsp. butter

Melt butter in pan. Add eggs and cheese. Cook until done.
Serves 2

Cheese Salad

1 tomato	1 lb. feta cheese
1 mushroom	1 lb. blue cheese
1 leaf of lettuce	1 lb. Parmesan
2 lb. cheddar	½ lb. Camembert
1 lb. Muenster	½ lb. Gruyère

Make everything bite-sized, then place in bowl. Serves 6 cheese-loving people.

Cheese Patties

6 lb. soft cheese

Form cheese into patties.
Serve on a bun.
Makes enough for 12 patties.

Cheese Pick-Me-Up

½ cup water
1 lb. Brie

Put everything in blender at a high speed. Serve immediately
Just enough for one

R. Chast

"*Last March, he cancelled his subscription to the Hillsburgh 'Weekly Clarion.'*
Currently he is an irate member of the Necktie-of-the-Month Club."

"That wasn't very nurturing of you."

"Reading left to right: That's me with my first wife. Then there's Mary, my second wife, and me. Then Linda, the children, and me. And the last one is just me at the Catskills."

"I know you don't agree with what I'm saying, son, but someday, when you're wealthier, you'll understand."

"Franklin can't discuss that—he's under constant electronic surveillance."

"May I remind you that here at Atherton, Pembroke & Wills we do <u>not</u> take fashion risks."

"I didn't actually <u>build</u> it, but it was based on my idea."

THESE POTATO CHIPS LOOK KIND OF FUNNY, TOM. I'M GOING TO RUN THEM DOWN TO THE LAB FOR TESTS.

SOME HOURS LATER IN THE THRONE ROOM...

A FEW MORE MINUTES, YOUR MAJESTY.

BETTER TO BE SAFE THAN SORRY, YOUR MAJESTY.

ZIEGLER

"Women kiss women good night. Men kiss women good night. But men do not kiss men good night—especially in Armonk."

Levin

"Fooling some of the people some of the time is good enough for me."

"Three bucks' worth of the regular, two bucks' worth of super-regular, and top it off with a buck's worth of high-test."

12 VARIATIONS

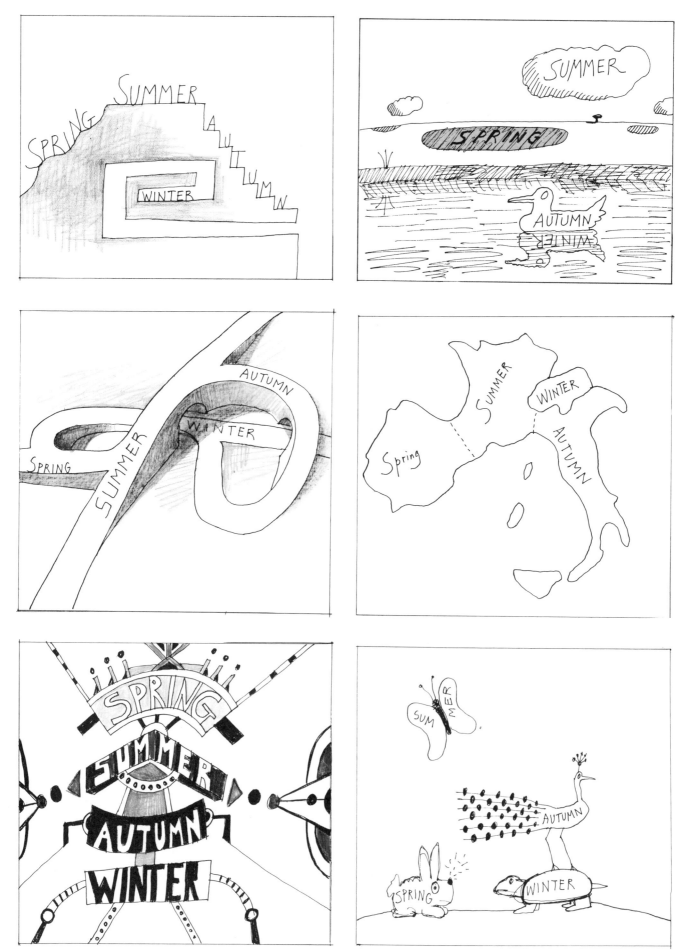

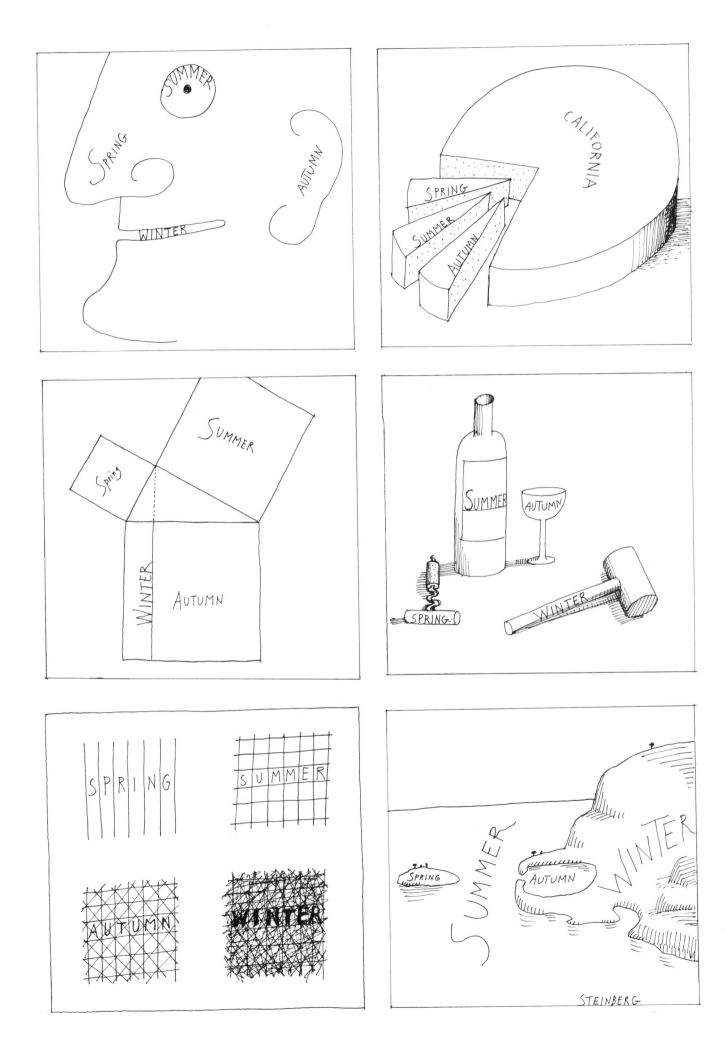

"*I'm going to level with you, Mom.*"

"Good morning, beheaded—uh, I mean beloved."

"<u>Wrong</u> <u>number?</u> This never happened with Ma Bell!"

"Tell me, sir, is there any such thing as just a plain
Republican, or are they all staunch?"

"Dearly beloved, we are gathered here yet again . . ."

"She wouldn't leave her name. Just said Room 14,
Hôtel Balzac, Rue de Seine, '34."

"Oh, sure, I've laid a few. But that was when gold was over seven hundred dollars an ounce."

"Why, Hennings, I had no idea."

"*Heavens, he's not worrying about his money, he's worrying about money itself.*"

"*Which of my points is 'moot'?*"

"*Murchison's theory is that it's dog hair in your fuel line.*"

"His Royal Highness was a night person."

"My Lord! Their basic house wine is the same as ours."

The Snowman Realizes Who He Is

"Don't you know some place with a mechanical bull?"

"You might as well take a seat, Mr. Gallagher. There's
a Reuben sandwich ahead of you."

"Darling, let's get divorced."

"If it please the Court, I have a
get-out-of-jail-free card."

"Oh, good!"

"I believe I'll skip the appetizer. I ate the flowers."

"Are you quoting the old Nixon or the new Nixon?"

"And now, having satisfied one hundred per cent of my daily requirements, I am returning to bed."

"I don't care if they *are* moving better over there. This is
the fast lane. This is where I live."

"Glad you brought that up, Jim. The latest research on polls has turned up some interesting variables. It turns out, for example, that people will tell you any old thing that pops into their heads."

"Damn it, Eddie! If you don't believe in nuclear war and you don't believe in conventional war, what the hell kind of war *do* you believe in?"

"I don't want any of this *soft* luggage. Show me some *hard* luggage!"

Lenin, Anticipating His Arrival at Finland Station,
Sees His Baggage Taken Off at Beloostrov

"I'll have the businesswoman's lunch."

"Good evening. I am Martha's son by a previous marriage."